Depth
of
Despair

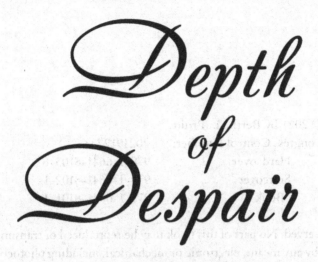

Depth
of
Despair

A Mother's Journal on
Schizophrenia

Bertha L. Pruitt

Copyright © 2021 by Bertha L. Pruitt.

Library of Congress Control Number:		2021912733
ISBN:	Hardcover	978-1-6641-8103-8
	Softcover	978-1-6641-8102-1
	eBook	978-1-6641-8101-4

Print information available on the last page.

Rev. date: 06/21/2021

To order additional copies of this book, contact:
Xlibris
844-714-8691
www.Xlibris.com
Orders@Xlibris.com
829811

1994

1994

The year was 1994; we arrived home around 3:00 p.m. from the hospital where my daughter, Dee, had spent one month as the result of a mental breakdown. After entering the house and dropping off her belongings in her room, I felt a need to go quickly to my room to privately thank God or, as she would say, the higher power for bringing her back from the pits of a bottomless hell. This had been the darkest and longest bout she had experienced with schizophrenia since being diagnosed some eighteen years earlier. This episode came exactly two years to the month of her last episode and strengthened the notion that episodes beget episodes.

If you are strong at heart, I invite you to come with me on this journey through sheer madness. This episode had taken a toll on my well-being. I who had always been strong. I who had always carried the load single-handedly. I who had never missed a day visiting her during her hospital stay. I, who had weathered many storms and had been able to conceal the pain and loss behind a mask of composure, was finally falling apart.

I reflected on the poem "Footprints" as the story goes, a man who had been faithful to God and noticed Christ walking beside him during his daily walks through life. One day he noticed only one set of footprints during his darkest moments. He questioned God, "Why aren't you ever there when I need you?"

Christ answered by saying, "When you saw only one set of prints, I was carrying you." Just as I, too, neared the limit of human endurance, James Cleveland's version of "Where Is Your Faith in God" became the force that kept me going.

My daughter suffers from one of the most devastating illnesses, but she has functioned at a very high level, sometimes to the point of maniac. In addition to working full-time, she had spent the past year and a half doing her practical to become a rehabilitation counselor. Since she was rarely home, I did not detect the behavior change until a friend of hers called to ask me if she had gone off her medications. Immediately, I feared the worst; she had switched to a new drug (Moban), which evidently did not work for her. A counselor she had been seeing at work was instrumental in getting her to see her doctor. Any attempt of intervention made by me was rejected as confrontational. She complied with the doctor's order to increase the dosage. After two days, something went terribly wrong and she stopped taking the medicine completely. Within a week, she was exhibiting all the symptoms of a major episode.

One evening, as I waited for her at the train station, I could not contain my tears, as she stepped off the train in the middle of the night wearing sunglasses. It is during periods like this that I worry about her most, wondering if something will happen to her while she is away from home. She had begun to function on about two hours of sleep nightly. No one else in the house could get much more, as she kept the boom box blasting, first with gospel music then rap.

I don't think she had slept at all since Friday when early Sunday morning she came into our bedroom and asked, "When are you going to call for the straightjacket (meaning the cops)?" In the past, each of her hospitalizations (five times) had been by force. She does not, or at least when she's in this frame of mind, realize how much easier and less expensive it would be if she would allow us to transport her to the hospital. She cannot conceive a voluntary commitment. So when she came to my room asking for help (really), I jumped at the opportunity and called the Department of Mental Health Crisis Intervention Center. I had spoken to someone there a few days earlier, seeking information on how they might assist in having her hospitalized rather than going through the police department, which had been so painful in the past. This being a Sunday morning, I got a different person on the telephone who did not think that the time had come to have her committed. You see, the law requires that the person has to be at the point of causing harm to self or someone else before they can intervene. I then called the local police department. They were very sympathetic but advised that they could not act without the pink slip (doctor's authorization). My next call was to the hospital where her doctor is on staff. I knew he was off on weekends, so I spoke with the doctor on duty. He was not familiar with her case. I finally convinced him that I needed help. After several calls between the doctor, the police department, and me, the wheel began to turn.

By time the ambulance arrived, my daughter was busy getting dressed and packing her things for a hospital stay. It came as no surprise that once the officers entered the house, she poked her head out of her room to ask if they had the pink slip. In all honesty, the officer said, "No, but we are working on it." "Fine," she said, "just let me know when you get it, and I will be ready." This necessitated more telephone calls between the officers and the station. When the order was finalized, the officer called out to her, "We are all set now." Again she came to the door and asked the officer if he would help her with her bags. By saying he would be delighted to assist, my daughter became more pleasant. They came out of her room carrying two large trash bags full of her belongings. In total disbelief, I could only comment, "My God, I guess she is going for the long haul."

Once at the local hospital (Norwood), she again became very uncooperative. She would not let the staff draw blood until half of the security force was present (she needed the authority figures around her), nor would she sign any papers. You, the reader, must understand that the complexity of a broken brain is such that this behavior is not unusual. This ordeal started around 7:00 a.m.; it was now noon, and she still had to be transported to the mental hospital. When she was finally admitted to the secure ward of the hospital and I was back home, I let out a sigh of relief, knowing that at last she was no longer exposed to the danger of the streets of Boston. However, I was not prepared for what was to follow. This turned out to be the longest and most painful experience of her eighteen years of mental illness. I began a journal:

Day 1 (December 13, 1994): She was acting strangely and did not give me a hug when I went to visit.

Day 2: She completely ignored me; she was totally consumed with reading a book on multiple personalities. She stated that she was refusing all contact with the outside world. No phone calls or visitors would be allowed. I left after 10 minutes.

Day 3: (no entry)

Day 4: Her father left for his holiday trip to Alabama. The family's cat of 19 years died. I continued my daily trips to the hospital.

Day 5: She would not let me come near her, stating that I had the smell of death about me and that her doctor was the devil. I learned from the staff that she had been forcibly injected because she was out of control. The medication did not abate her condition as it had done in the past. She would only talk to me if I kept the focus on me. If I asked a question about her, she quickly terminated the visit. After a few days, her condition had deteriorated to the point where she refused to get dressed, comb her hair, or leave her room. She refused the food and water at the hospital and got a charge out of ordering me to bring certain things, saying if I wanted guardianship of her (at age 36) I would have to earn it. Daily, I took water, fruit, and seafood salad to her. If the seafood salad was not purchased at Stop & Shop Supermarket, she would refuse it.

The weather was the worst we had had in many years. On several occasions, the staff commented on how they didn't know how I could make the trip every day. They didn't say it, but I am sure they meant since my visits meant nothing to my daughter anyhow. Dee (my daughter) was well contented to read, stare at the walls, and have an occasion conversation with herself. Here her cries were not heard, her laughter not shared. She did not acknowledge my presence when I opened the door to her room. With a heavy heart, after a few moments, I just closed the door and went back home to prepare for our traditional family get-together at my home. Hidden behind my mask, I got through the evening. After everyone left, I cried for hours, just me alone in the empty house, no family, not even my cat.

On December 25 (Christmas morning), a cousin called and said she wanted to go with me to the hospital. I tried to prepare her for the worst without telling her that she shouldn't go. She and Dee were very close, so I prayed that at least Dee would visit with her—not so. When we arrived, Dee became extremely angry and stated something about her right to refuse visitors. Again, we left.

On December 27, I was informed by staff that she had begun to eat a little better—at least they had observed her at the refrigerator several times.

On December 30, a court hearing was scheduled for 3:00 p.m. to force appropriate treatment. I arrived at 2:15 p.m., hoping to see a faint ray of my daughter in the monster she had become. While she still refused to speak to me, the hearing went very well. Her only remark was for clarification that the neuroleptics would be by force. The judge assured her that since it was court ordered, that certainly was by force. She was very relieved and went directly to the nurses' station to get her meds upon return to the ward. She was told that it would take about one-half hour to clear up the paperwork and all. I stayed with her to ensure that everything went well. After waiting a few minutes, she became anxious and kept asking, "What time is it?" An hour passed; there were changing of the guards, still no medication. She was becoming more and more hostile and agitated. When they finally came to administer the injection, all hell broke loose. I was asked to wait in the cafeteria. After twenty minutes, I went back to the ward. I was told by one of the nurses that she was in restraints. The nurse's expression suggested that I should not attempt to see her that night. So I walked straight past my daughter's room and asked to be let out of the locked ward. In my distress, I heard someone say, "You can call back later." When I called later that evening, I was told that she would be okay.

On December 31, my telephone rang at 8:30 a.m. It was Dee; she suggested without apologizing (as she had always done in the past) that maybe she had been rude to me. I knew this was out of character for her, but I was just overjoyed that she was on the right track. Her mood had changed by time I visited that afternoon. She sat reading a book without much enthusiasm about my visit. This behavior was totally foreign from her past episodes. I suddenly became drained again, as it appeared that the medication was having no effect. I feared that the latest episode had altered her brain to the point that it could no longer respond to previously effective drugs. At this point, I was ready to try anything, including exorcism, when a friend called and offered to fast with me. I was not in the habit of fasting but was willing to try, as I was reminded of the song "Where Is Your Faith in God."

1995

1995

On January 1, 1995, my friend and I successfully completed our commitment of fasting and praying. That afternoon, I met with the social worker who inquired about my well-being and how I managed to visit each day. I am sure she also meant since my visits meant very little to Dee. I smiled and said, "As painful as it is, it is something I have to do." The social worker nodded her head as if she understood.

In Dee's twisted mind, I was serving a purpose, earning my right to guardianship, which I did not have but she didn't know that. Each day when I arrived, she had another list of things for me to do or pick up. Without any form of greeting, she would start with, "Did you do this or so?" I was baffled by her lack of improvement. Her doctor also confided that he, too, did not understand it. I began dreading when family members inquired about her condition. The questions always were, "What did the doctor say?" or "Why don't they change the medication?" I could only sigh and say, "How can anyone know what goes on in someone's mind, especially a mind that is so tormented?" By now, I was fully convinced that her condition was beyond man and only God or the higher power could unscramble her broken brain. There were no blood tests or urine samples to produce a proper diagnosis, medication, or treatment. Following the above entries, the daily entries in my journal became the same: "Please, God, help me" or "Please don't leave me now."

On January 3, 1995, her father had arrived back home and made his first visit to the hospital. He was completely ignored—for this, I felt terrible, as he cannot or does not know how to cope with this illness. After that, he rarely asked about her. One day he announced that he could not bear to see her in that condition. To myself, I thought, *Well, what about me?*

On January 13, 1995, one month after her admission, I discovered that she had ground privileges, which meant she could sign out to leave the ward to visit the cafeteria and other areas of the hospital. She began to make a few telephone calls but still refused to allow visitors. She informed me that she might get an off-grounds pass that coming weekend. She wanted to know how I felt about it. I said "Great" while deep inside I had my doubts, as she certainly was not herself. When she didn't call early the next morning, my heart did a pitty-pat. When I visited that afternoon, her spirit was down; she didn't mention the pass. When I inquired, she stated, "If it's to be it will be." Later that evening, her doctor called to get my input on the upcoming pass. We both recognized that her spirit was not up to par. The doctor told me that he would approve the pass for the next day (which was Saturday) but if I did not feel after seeing her that she should go, I could just refuse to take her.

On Saturday morning (10:00 a.m.), I picked her up at the hospital for a four-hour visit. It was apparent that she was not herself and that I would have to walk on eggshells. She barely said "Hi" to her father when we arrived home. She took a bath and changed clothes but still refused to comb her hair (dreadlocks); we took off for the mall where she did a little shopping. On the drive back to the hospital, she said that she wanted to go to church the next day (Sunday). I informed her that she would have to come home first to get dressed for church. Her intention was to go as she was. I, who was brought up with the notion that one must wear their Sunday finest to the Lord's house, had to risk an argument with her and say that I could not possibly take her to church dressed like that. Her reply was, "Okay, we won't go." End of discussion. When she signed back in at the hospital, she was told to answer the questions on the release form. This was meant to be therapeutic in nature. The first question was, Why were you given a pass? She simply wrote "To go around," evidence of disjointed thinking.

On January 16, 1995 (Sunday morning), I went to the hospital to pick Dee up at noon. There had been no improvement in her state of mind, except that she was looking forward to visiting the Haitian family next door, who was preparing an African dish for her lunch. I offered to drop her off next door out of fear for her safety and to ensure that she had no other intentions. She insisted on walking, so I hid behind the curtains and watched from my window. About thirty minutes later, I decided to go for a walk in spite of the subzero weather. Subconsciously, I also headed to the neighbor's house. As I walked in, I noticed this strange or different look in Dee's eyes. I thought, *Oh my God, she is angry that I followed her.* The neighbor said, "We were just about to call you." Dee jumped up to give me a big hug. Coming out of the delusion and disturbance in thoughts, she said, "Mom, I thought you were part of a satanic cult who could hear and read my thoughts at the hospital, but Monique has explained that is impossible as only God has that ability." I was dumbfounded; instantly, the monster had been transformed. I had my daughter back. She called her father to say that she

13

was better. We rushed home; she began calling everyone and apologizing for the prior six weeks. When I dropped her back at the hospital, she asked that I do not say anything to the staff, but the gleam in her eyes gave her away. As we were let back onto the ward, a couple of the nurses who were leaving their shift exclaimed, "Wow, what a change. We see that you had a great visit today." Her appearance had improved 100 percent. I had combed her hair and braided it into two cornrows. She began to greet all the staff and fellow clients, whom she had not spoken to during her entire stay.

What a coincidence, the movie *Out of Darkness*, starring Diana Ross, aired that same night. I was so relieved that this would be a great educational tool for those who had not experienced the heartaches of this terrible disease. I could not contain the tears as I sat glued to the screen. Here on national television was a true picture of the exact ordeal my daughter and I had just endured. I really lost it in the scene where Diana was put into restraints, lying on the bed spread-eagle, with both arms and legs strapped down. While this was unbearably graphic, it did not compare with what it was like for Dee who had refused to put on any clothing. The movie clearly demonstrated the ignorance of the public and the high intelligence of those afflicted with the disease.

Two days later, Dee was ready to be released from the hospital. I arrived before her doctor made his rounds to sign the release forms. Briefly, I indicated to the doctor that I was not sure that it was the medication that turned her around. He was 100 percent sure that it was. He spoke from a scientific viewpoint, as my son who is a pharmacist had done the night before during our telephone conversation. I did not pursue my theory, as I do not possess the qualification or understanding to explain the effects of antipsychotic drugs on the targeted dopamine (D-2, 3, 4, 7) receptors of the brain. I only know that God is.

On May 11, 1995, the first sign of more problems, Dee announced that she would not be going to Alabama with us this year to what had become an annual trip for her father's family reunion. The next day, in an effort to prevent another hospitalization, I had her prescription refilled, but she refused to take the medication.

May 14 (Mother's Day): I had been getting little sleep. To wake on such a beautiful morning with pains that eat away at the soul. After praying for a miracle, I found only a void and the will to put into words the following poem:

To Lose a Child to Mental Illness

The greatest gift for a mother on Mother's Day
Is the healing of her child's broken mind in a
miraculous way.
Her prayer is for a cure of the dreadful disease,
Which stole her child's mind at an early age
While leaving a physical frame to be cursed at
and blamed.
In an evil world bursting with shame, only a
mother can
Feel this throbbing pain.

Her prayer is for guidance and a helping hand,
While in reality she knows nothing will ever be
the same.

Yet she continues to hope for a breakthrough in
medical
Science to free her child's mind during her
lifetime.
What a joy it would be and peace sublime
To awake from this nightmare knowing her
child has
Eternal care.

Bersy, 1995

May 15, 1995: This was a fairly quiet day. I called the doctor to schedule an appointment for Dee. She wants help but cannot bring herself to make that move.

May 16, 1995: She is looking forward to visiting her doctor. We arrived early. After a few minutes, she begins to lose a grip on reality. She becomes increasingly disruptive and loud, speaking to everyone in the waiting room and showering me with hugs. Her visit with the doctor lasted about five minutes. She informed him that she is not taking any drugs (prescribed medication); she agreed to go to the hospital (Westwood Lodge). Her doctor advised that I (her mom) should drive. She went along peacefully, as she was trying her best to be cooperative. She even commented that this was the first time she was not being transported by the Men in Blue. When we arrived at Westwood Lodge Admission, we had a very long wait in a dismal surrounding. How I wished we didn't have to be there. Dee was quite upbeat and talkative with the caregiver that came for her. She was quite contented to be back in her old and familiar surroundings. She settled right in, sat down, and started chatting with the few lost souls that were roaming around. I wrote down the public telephone number for the ward and headed home so very tired and mentally exhausted. I climbed into bed and fell asleep. I woke up at midnight—took a pen and started writing.

Day 3: In a small way, I was informed of a ray of hope. Dee informed me that she had taken an injection. I prayed that it would continue. The next day, I was hoping that the phone would ring with encouraging news. By ten o'clock, I began to lose hope. But I continued in prayer.

On May 20 and 21, 1995 (Saturday and Sunday), there was nothing to record in my journal, except "No improvement from medication."

On May 22 (Monday), Dee dropped the bomb; she was refusing all meds and was looking forward to her day in court.

On May 23 (Tuesday), I called an attorney for information/procedures on guardianship. The attorney said he would get right on the case. It seemed that the doctor was concerned about vital signs. The next day at 8:45 a.m., I received a call from the attorney. They had already held court. I was slated for a 1:00 p.m. appointment with a social worker. Dee did not attend the meeting. When I stopped by the ward to visit Dee, she seemed relieved that "the man had ordered the drugs." As I stated earlier, she would not comply on her own. Through all this, she stated that she would not lose her cool this time. She displayed no anger, and I could only say, "Thank You, God."

On May 25, 1995, at 10:15 p.m., my niece Carolyn called to check on things. I had previously shared my writing of earlier episodes with her. I was touched by her concern and timing, as Pruitt (Dee's father) had just left for a trip to Alabama. He did

17

not inquire about Dee, and I did not tell him that her condition was not good and her vital signs were fluctuating. When I visited her earlier in the day, her doctor was trying to impress on her the need to eat and drink or they would have to start an IV. I also received a shipment of books in the mail today from a woman I met on a trip to Africa. I was very grateful, for this would keep me occupied for a while.

On May 26, at 8:00 a.m., I returned from an early morning walk and discovered the following message from my daughter:

> "Mom, I am better now. Come to see me. Come real early. Sorry for giving you such a rough time. Come to see me, but don't call. I don't want to answer the phone."

At 8:30 a.m., I received another call. She said, "Mom, guess what? I am much better. This is a strange disease. They increased my medication, and I am much better. I am going to ask for a pass today for a cookout that's being held here on Monday (Memorial Day). Do you want to come?" I was much relieved and said, "Thank You, God!"

The weekend went well. She had a three-hour visit on Saturday and five hours on Sunday. On Monday, Memorial Day, her cousin and I attended the cookout at the hospital. It rained, so we ate in the cafeteria.

On May 30, 1995, when I returned from my morning walk, there was a message to call her around 9:00 a.m. I called and was told to come pick her up as she had been discharged. Back home, as we unloaded the car, I noticed a bird in its nest between the gutter pipe and the wall near my front door. I thought, *How brave.* A few days earlier, a baby rabbit had run across my front steps. He had been eating the flowers next to the steps. Right away, I recognized a lesson of faith from these creatures; consider the birds of the air, the lilies of the field, and the animals of the wild. God looks after them. Surely He will do likewise for us.

On June 4 or 5, Dee returned to work part-time. I received a call from a coworker of hers (a Christian lady) telling me what a blessing that I had picked up on the onset of another episode in its early stages. She told me of my daughter's love for me. I needed that reinforcement. Coping with mental illness is so draining on all involved.

On June 12, 1995, a niece was also exhibiting symptoms of mental illness. Dee was aware of this and asked if I was aware of her cousin's condition. I was aware but felt I could not deal with any more at that time. After a while, I decided to intercede and encouraged the niece to seek help.

1999

1999

Things went well for the next four years. On April 22, 1999, I was called away to Saginaw, Michigan, where my mother's life was fading away and my oldest sister was in a nursing home. I spent two and a half days in Michigan before I had to rush back to Boston on Sunday, April 25; I was scheduled to return on April 29. I thought things were fine when I left home (4:00 a.m.), but I didn't get an answer when I called back that night. I called again at eight the next morning and was greeted by a monster of a daughter. I could not believe my ears. She had been transformed from light to darkness in a matter of hours. When I reached my husband that night, he informed me that Dee was not doing well and had left for a planned trip to Pennsylvania to attend a Free Jamal rally.

I arrived back in Boston around 1:00 p.m. on Sunday; Dee had got in around 2:00 a.m. earlier that day. She was headed out the door when I arrived and did not wish to hear anything from me. She went to work on Monday totally consumed in her disturbed state. Early Tuesday, I received a call from her supervisor. I was relieved to hear from her, as I was in the process of trying to reach her. The supervisor told me that they were transporting Dee to her doctor's office. The doctor's assessment was that she could come home, so I picked her up from the doctor's office.

I realized right away that she had become a real terror. During the drive home and the entire evening, she verbally abused me like never before. The twenty years of dealing with the disease had not prepared me for this behavior.

I knew that she was consumed by the disease, but my upbringing made it hard for me to accept some of the profanity that she dished out. She finally fell asleep.

On April 28, 1999, around 7:15 a.m., I overheard her on the telephone making plans to go out. She reminded me that she had refused her medication the night before and would continue without being drugged up. I feared for her safety and decided I had to try and stop her, so I stole away and called the police department and Southwood Hospital. Again, they went through the process of telling me that their hands were tied. I then placed an emergency call to her doctor, who tried to convince her to take her medication. She absolutely refused but agreed to come in to his office. I drove her to the office without any fanfare. It seemed that she was asking to be committed to the hospital. She suggested to her doctor that she would be locked up like her brothers in jail (reference to the Free Jamal rally she attended in Pennsylvania). The doctor made arrangements to have her committed. Dee suggested that she would be transported by "the system" via ambulance. While we waited for the ambulance to arrive, Dee was very relaxed, talking with her doctor who had recently returned to the US after being out of the country a couple of years.

She again made a list of things that I should bring to her at the hospital.

I rushed home and packed a bag for her and dashed off to Westwood Lodge. I was alarmed at how much the facility had deteriorated. Dee was sitting in the dayroom reading.

On April 30, 1999, I arrived at the hospital to learn that Dee had been placed in seclusion for assaulting a patient and a nurse. As I turned to leave the building, before the door closed, Dee ran out of her room swearing. I heard her say, "I will see you, Mom." Somehow, I found the strength to keep going. I called Michigan to check on my mother and was told there had been no change. At 6:00 p.m., I called my daughter's hospital again, but I was given no information because of the confidentiality clause. I asked to have the doctor call me. So at 9: 15 p.m., I received a call from the doctor who told me that she was still in seclusion, having refused to take medication. The hospital was trying to get a Rogers (authorization from the court), which would take some time; meanwhile, they would have to forcibly medicate if needed.

On May 1, 1999, when I visited the hospital, I found a very angry and drugged-up monster. There was no communication between us.

On May 2 (Sunday), I went back to the hospital to take personal items for Dee. Upon hearing my voice in the hallway, she ran out of her room screaming at me. She would only accept the Koran (Muslim Bible) from the items I brought her (most of which she had demanded that I bring). I was there less than five minutes. I went on to an awards banquet at Northeastern University and an annual candlelight service at my church. Around eleven that night, I received a phone call from Dee saying she was much better, and she asked if I could visit her at that hour. She said that she was using her calling card and hiding in a closet to make the call. I am sure that she meant an enclosed phone booth. In any event, I cried out, "*Thank You, God.*" I told her I would see her in the morning.

On May 3 (Monday), at 8:00 a.m., she called again to say she was fine and to find out what time I would visit. The visit went well.

On May 4, she called to see if I could make an 11:00 a.m. meeting with her new doctor and case manager (her longtime doctor was no longer at Westwood Lodge). The new doctor and case manager were busy making arrangements for her release on Friday. Dee indicated that she would see her original doctor at his office on Thursday.

On May 5, I received several calls; Dee was being released that day. She wanted to know what time I could pick her up. We agreed on 2:00 p.m., as I was attending an appreciation luncheon for volunteers at Medfield State Hospital. She was waiting for me at the door when I arrived. We both left the hospital feeling very upbeat. Certainly, God is good.

The next day, I drove her to her appointment with her regular doctor. He was amazed that she had made such a remarkable comeback. He asked if I thought she was okay. I said somewhat, as she was still totally consumed with a college course she was taking and felt that she had to make class on Saturday. I must add that going to school in addition to working full-time was the manifestation of her maniac condition.

May 7 was a sad day for me; I had a burning sensation in the pit of my stomach. I knew that I had to let go and let God take control. I had done my best, but Mom was still very sick.

May 8—I almost hated to face the day. Dee had been up since 1:00 a.m. working on a school assignment; she worked on it until 10:30 a.m. I knew this was a bit intense for her fragile mind, but there was nothing I could do about it. She drove herself to class and called back and left a message that she had made it safely. She called again at 2:30 p.m. en route home.

On May 9 (Mother's Day), my entry to the journal was to say "All is well."

On May 10 (Monday), Dee and I went to a Legal Sea Foods restaurant for lunch.

On May 11, I received a call from Michigan; Mom was gone.

Dee kept it together while I went to Alabama for my mother's funeral. There were no further entries in my journal.

2001

2001

Dee's next episode came in November 2001. I first noticed her unusual behavior on November 3. A few days later, I called her doctor to notify him. She continued to go to work. I was trying to reach her new supervisor, whom I did not know. On November 10 (Friday), I called an ex-supervisor (a woman who attended the same church as me and was quite familiar with Dee). I missed her at work but reached her at home that night. I wanted to alert them, as they had been so helpful throughout her illness. I also knew that her coworkers were afraid of her when she was in a crisis. At 12:30 p.m., I received a call from her supervisor, who had been trying to reach me. These people were at a loss, and I truly felt bad that they had to be subjected to this, but I had no control over Dee, and in no way could I keep her home from work. At 4:00 p.m., her ex-manager called to say that Dee had been dismissed from work and she had promised them she would come home. After she had not arrived around 5:30 p.m., I began to fear and wondered where she would have gone. I decided to look for her at the gym. She had taken to visiting the gym after work and had a tremendous weight loss (this is also a manifestation of the disease). She was not there. Around 8:30 p.m., she arrived home very angry. She told me that she had been dismissed from work and suggested that if I were going to call the f—— cops, I should do it now while she was still dressed. I jumped at the offer. When Qfficer Simmons arrived, he didn't have a clue about what was transpiring. He called for assistance. Another car arrived; they decided that she could be transported without a pink slip since she agreed to go quietly. In her twisted thinking, she was alert enough to know that she didn't want to be transported by ambulance. She had to pay out of pocket the last time (smart girl—crazy yet wise).

She went quietly in the patrol car, while Pruitt and I followed in our car. After waiting a while in the emergency room, Dee became very agitated and uncooperative. On call was a doctor that Dee knew from church. The doctor managed to convince Dee to let them take her temperature and blood pressure. She informed them that no blood work would be allowed. If you have been to emergency in a busy hospital, you are aware of what the waiting is like. It was around 2:30 a.m. before the crisis team gave their report after contacting the insurance company. Norwood Hospital was not in the network, so Dee was to be transported to Westwood Lodge. We were told that we could go home, so we didn't wait around to see the scene of them trying to get into an ambulance, as she had taken a stand that she would not pay the cost (again that smart portion of the brain at work).

On Saturday, at 1:00 p.m., I went over to Westwood Lodge with clothing for her. She declined to see me, so I left the package at the desk. I called on Sunday. She was still refusing visitors. On Monday, November 12, I again went in person. I was admitted to the ward. Dee was still angry and rude. I visited a few minutes with another patient and left. My only consolation was thinking, *Thank God, at least she is safe.* On November 13, I did not visit the hospital but spoke with a case manager, the doctor in charge at Westwood Lodge, and her personal doctor, who was no longer at Westwood. I was desperately seeking to have her medicated. Again, we went through the requirement procedures. Nothing could be done without a Rogers (court order), which could take a week or more, when the judge would make an on-site visit. The only consolation in this was that the judge would see her in the throes of the disease. I could only pray for strength to keep going. For the next few days, I could not visit; the social worker told me we must respect the wishes of the client. Only a mother can imagine the heartaches this disease causes. This was the first time I was not allowed to visit; even after being thrown out, I would show up the next day. I knew how disruptive this was to the other clients and staff.

On Friday, I stopped by the attorney's office to begin the temporary guardianship process. Only the secretary was in; she promised to have someone call me. Late afternoon, no one had called, and I was nearing the end of my rope, thinking the next day was her birthday. I had to do something to try to reach her. So I brought flowers and fruit to the hospital, which I left at the desk. It was much later that I remembered it was only November 17 and her birthday was November 20.

The next two days, I heard nothing from her. I received a call from the attorney's office to inform me that they were doing a feasibility of an outpatient Rogers for November 20. After returning from the gym that day, I found a message from the doctor requesting to see me prior to the hearing. After meeting with the doctor, I went to the cafeteria to wait for the hearing to start. I was recognized by Dee's appointed attorney, who had been unable to meet with her due to her agitated state of mind. We had a nice chat and went into the hearing room. Dee was ushered in yelling "Racist, racist, and racist" as she pointed to each person in the room. When she pointed to me, she yelled "Get her the f—— out of here" as she stormed out. I left the room; she went back in and stormed out again after a few minutes. This time she was escorted back to the locked ward. The judge stated that I could come back into the room to hear the testimony from the doctor. There was no opposition, so the hearing was over in no time. The doctor informed me that I was free to leave; it was over, and the only thing left was for the judge to sign the papers. Her appointed attorney and I walked back to the parking lot together. As luck would have it, he was a very religious man and offered to pray for my daughter. He had three daughters—8, 7, and 5; they all were involved in his ministry and had interceded on many people's behalf. To me this was *special*. At seven that night, I called the ward and was told that Dee had agreed to take her medications and was taking physical as we spoke. This was encouraging, but I would know for sure when she decide to call me. "Happy birthday. She was now age forty-two."

November 21: I had been praying for a miracle. No call. A beautiful bouquet of flowers was delivered from her coworkers. I called the hospital and was told it was not a good idea to come over. She was still very sick.

On November 22 (Thanksgiving Day), I prayed that God would remove that stronghold of anger from my child. I was afraid to call the hospital to inquire of her condition. At 2:30 p.m., my son called; he had just called the hospital and was shocked to discover that Dee refused to take the call. He could hear her in the background swearing and being very abusive. Her father left for Alabama today. Again, the whole load was on me.

On November 23, I noted in my dairy that only a mother could possibly comprehend the agony of seeing a loved one totally out of control. I called the hospital; both the doctor and nurse were off. I spoke to someone on the ward who informed me that Dee had a very bad day. She was being very disruptive and combatable, which they "don't tolerate there." Well, what did she mean by that? I knew how difficult it was for everyone there, but what could be gained from a remark like that being spoken to a heartbroken mom? Lord, please unscramble that twisted mind.

November 25: report, status quo.

On November 26, I received a call from her doctor, who found that her condition had deteriorated since he last saw her (Wednesday before Thanksgiving). She would not allow him in the room. Her medication had increased from 5mg of Haldol to 10mg over the weekend, and he was thinking of increasing it to 15mg. I tried to go about my day as best as I could. I rushed home, hoping that somehow there would be a message from her on my line. No such luck. I decided to review her last admission in 1995. I felt a bit better after seeing that she had been hospitalized six weeks at that time. I decided I would call her original doctor the next day. Meanwhile, I received a call from the Disability Claims dDepartment from her job—requesting to speak to her. Because of confidentiality and whatnot, they could not speak with me. I gave her the telephone number to the hospital. After a few minutes, she called back to say everything was okay and Dee's benefits were covered through December 3. I placed a call to Ms. Brown (her supervisor) to see if this was a new procedure. She was not available, and she called me later that night. She apologized for the call from the central office and said that in the future she would try to satisfy the request. She also confirmed that it was her department that sent the flowers. Thank God for such caring people.

It was now 11:00 p.m.; alone and depressed, I was ready for bed, with a ray of hope that I just might get that call tomorrow.

On November 27, 2001, I went to the hospital to take her some clothing. I was told at the entrance that she was calm right now, so they didn't want to upset her, as the other patients were fearful of her. So I left without seeing her. I left a message for her original doctor that there had been no improvement.

November 28 was a very disturbing day. I called the unit around 3:00 p.m. I was transferred to a *doctor's voice mail*. I found this to be quite unacceptable. So I called the unit again. The person answering the phone tried to explain the law. In the heart and mind of a driven mother, there is no law. I was told that someone would contact me.

On November 29, at 8:20 a.m., I called the case manager's line. She had not arrived yet. She returned my call around 8:50 a.m. She, too, was restricted by the *law*, but she did share that there had been a slight improvement in her condition. At least she had taken the medication without restraints the night before. She also thought that the medication was being increased. Dee was still very, very angry. I left a message for the doctor to call me. When I returned home from an errand, there was a message from the doctor saying that he had met with her. Thing were encouraging, but there was still a long way to go.

On November 30, at 6:45 a.m., my sister called to see how things were going. I told her I had not been able to visit lately.

She didn't understand that and told me I should go to make sure she was okay. I agreed. I sighed to myself, *If she only knew what price I would willingly pay for the opportunity to set foot in her room.* I called the ward to see if I could visit and was told maybe within a couple of days. Deep within, I knew there had been little improvement or Dee would have certainly called herself. Each time I left the house, I would rush back to check my messages.

On December 1, I received no word from my child. Her father returned from Alabama.

On December 2 (Sunday), I called the public phone on the unit; while I was on hold, someone hung up.

On December 3, at 7:00 a.m., I received that long-awaited call. "Hi, Mom. I am much better." I received several more calls that day; she was busy planning her recovery strategy with the case manager, and I met with both of them later that day. Dee was very happy with the case manager. I called my sister to give her a report.

December 4—what a difference a day makes. I received no call. I knew things were not good. I went over to visit; she had a casual visit with me but refused to see her social worker. I offered to leave some change so she could make some phone calls. She declined, saying there would be no calls. It is impossible to explain this terrible disease.

On December 5, at 7:00 a.m., she was back on schedule; she called to say that she was better and wanted to know what time could I visit. She was allowed outside privileges, so we went out to shoot a few baskets. She had encouraged another patient to ask me for eight dollars for transportation home to Worcester. I thank God for each moment that I can do something good!

On December 6, Dee called early to say all was well. After I returned home from doing errands, there was a message from her case manager: "Dee is being discharged." When I went to pick her up, I sensed I must walk on thin ice. We stopped at the drugstore to get her prescriptions filled. The pharmacist wouldn't fill the prescriptions because of counterattack of the two drugs (Haldol and Geodon). I am not sure just what happened, but I did get the prescriptions later. She was becoming increasingly hyper, but she took the meds without too much fuss.

On December 7 (Friday), what started out as a beautiful beginning turned into my worst nightmare. She was scheduled to report back to the hospital for day treatment. She left home as scheduled for the 9:30 a.m. treatment plan but never showed up at the hospital. I was not aware of this as I went about my day; I did not arrive home until 3:00 p.m., and I discovered a message from the hospital that Dee had not shown up. I spoke with a Ms. Sullivan at the hospital. Evidently, they were highly concerned; she immediately notified the Walpole Police Department and the Newton-Wellesley Hospital, where Dee's doctor was on staff. I was instructed to go to the station to fill out a missing person report. It was now about 7:00 p.m.—no word from Dee. What a nightmare! 3:00 a.m.—still no word; I decided I had to try to get some sleep. Lord, it's in your hand!

At 7:00 a.m. on Saturday, the phone rang; it was Dee, calling to tell me that she had left her car parked in front of my nephew's house in Dorchester. She refused to say where she was and hung up. I called my nephew to confirm that the car was there. I then called my other niece to say that I had heard from Dee and that

I was coming in to the city to pick up the car. They drove out to my house instead and picked up the keys. My nephew even drove through the city looking for her (via Blue Hill Avenue). I notified the police department that the car had been found. I took photos of her to the station to run on the wires. They must have suggested it earlier, but they were now saying that it was out of their area.

Just as I got back home, the phone was ringing. It was Dee, saying, "Mom, don't you know where I am? I am at Rosie's Place (a homeless shelter for women). I am here for lunch after spending the night at Pine Street Inn (another shelter)." I called my niece to pick her up there. Somehow I was able to keep her on the phone until they arrived. She was in her element with the homeless population. In fact, my niece and nephew found her outside greeting the people as they arrived for lunch. They waited with her until she could pick up her belongings at the inn. Unbeknownst to me, she had packed a bag and sneaked it into her car before she left home Friday morning. Meanwhile, her dad, who worked in the city, called to check on things. I asked him to pick Dee up at my niece's home instead of having them make another trip to my home, which was twenty-plus miles away. I don't know how I would have made it without the family's help. We all retired early that night. We had our first snow for the season. I hoped that was an indication that the day would be washed off the slate *forever*!

Things went well the following week as I drove her back and forth to her day treatment program. By the weekend, she was getting itchy for her car, which we had left at my niece's home. She began to get bitchy and very confrontational. We brought the car home that Saturday, and she was in a better mood but was having a difficult time trying to regulate her medications and hook up with a counselor. We spent time together food shopping, and we visited a craft store, where she purchased some candles. Later that afternoon, she went out alone. I was ready to panic again when she was not back by dark. Having gone through such a devastating experience, I don't think I will ever relax again. She called around 8:00 p.m. to report that she was at the shopping mall. She arrived home at 9:00 p.m. loaded down with packages, a true symptom of maniac behavior. Still, God is good!

2010

2010

May 27, 2010: Dear Lord, I won't complain. It has been a while since I walked this journey. It caught me by surprise. We left for Alabama on Friday, May 21, 2010, to bury my sister Hazel who had expired suddenly. My first glimpse of trouble was when we arrived at the airport in Birmingham, Alabama. She had always done the driving from the airport to our home one hundred miles away, but in the rental car, she informed me that I should take over the driving so I would learn how to do it on my own. jeez, what a shocker, but we made it without fanfare. Thank You, God! Once we arrived, she took on a different personality. My sisters from Michigan were staying with us. My child was anything but her usually warm self. She informed them that she had a hair across her butt and wished to be left alone. She did not attend the funeral that Saturday and stated that she was only taking care of herself. She insisted on driving the car, which made me very nervous as the unfamiliar roads in Alabama are quite different for driving. We were able to agree on returning home to Boston. The flights were scheduled for Tuesday, May 25. My sisters were also scheduled to return to Michigan that day.

Thank God, we made it home safely. Still, my daughter was unreachable. The next day, she dashed off in her car around

11:00 a.m. She would not reveal where she was going, only "to take care of personal business." She returned home around 3:30 p.m. with a new haircut—and the police to transport her to the emergency room at the hospital. Meanwhile, I had called her doctor to issue the necessary paperwork. She refused to be transported by ambulance but went willingly in the police cruiser after warning me not to show up there or make any attempts to see her (but I went to the hospital anyway). She refused to cooperate with admission procedures and was held in emergency overnight. The next day was spent trying to gather the essential information. At 1:30 p.m., I checked with Riverside (admitting office) to learn that they had submitted the necessary info to the insurance company and were now waiting to hear from them. She was finally admitted around 4:00 p.m. I spoke with the nurse on the ward around 7:00 p.m. I was told that Dee wanted to speak with me; she asked me to come right over to visit. When I arrived, she was back to normal. She even called her dad, and things seemed fine.

The next day, Friday (May 28)—what a letdown from the evening before. She had requested that I bring two oranges, slippers, and books. When I arrived, her anger was not quite as forceful as before, but certainly not very nice. She sat with me about two minutes and decided she needed her space. She was going to have the social worker help her find an apartment so she could get away from us. I had also brought her a change of clothes, which she refused to take so I ended up bringing them back home. Lord, I knew this day had been too good to last.

On Saturday (May 29, 2010), when I checked with the desk, I was told that Dee wanted to see me—yes, along with a list of things to bring: five pairs of panties (size 12) and a bar of soap.

I added an extra bra, which she had indicated she wanted (the day before), only to bring it back home. Upon my arrival, she was standing near the nurses' station as if waiting for me. The bag was checked and given to her. She preceded to her room to ensure that I had followed her instructions. Once that was done, I was told I could leave. The entire visit was approximately five minutes.

On Sunday (May 30, 2010), I went to church locally and decided I would call before I visit. She refused to come to the phone. Later I received a call from a social worker seeking more information on her psychological history. The social worker informed me that nothing much would be done over the holiday weekend. So I had another restless night.

On Monday (May 31, 2010), I made a call to the pay phone unit; she refused to take the call. Later that day, I called the nurses' unit to be told that there had been no changes. She was refusing meds and any form of participation. I would just have to wait it out and see what would happen on Tuesday. I was praying for God's mercy. I realized how difficult this must be on her psychic.

On Tuesday (June 1, 2010), no visit and contact with a social worker or doctor. Everything was a repeat of past history.

On Wednesday (June 2), I was to the ward. per (by her request. Thursday) I met with the social worker and doctor. This being a new set of people required an update on past history. Lord, I am so worn, having to repeat the same things over and over.

Thursday, June 3—what a trying day this had been, having to process the medical information for Verizon (her employer). Everyone was using the confidential aspects. I was also informed that a hearing would not transpire until next Wednesday. This drove me over the edge. I went wild! I requested a meeting with all department(s) heads. Hearings were held on Wednesdays, so I could not understand why the hearing was not done yesterday.

Dee had already been there for a week and by now was totally insane. All communication with me had been cut. The poor girl was totally insane by now. I contacted Atty. James Hilliard, an attorney I had used in the past, to see if he could get the hearing date moved forward. He called back to say he was trying but things didn't look too hopeful.

Lord, what am I to do?

The next few days (Friday, Saturday, and Sunday) were a sheer nightmare for me). Late Sunday evening, after being unable to contain myself any longer, I called the nurses' unit to see if my daughter, Dee, would see me. After relaying the message, the nurse came back on the line and said, "She said *no* along with a few choice words."

On Monday (June 7, 2010), at 7:20 a.m., the phone rang; it was Dee. "Hi, Mom, can you hear me? I am much better today." She had taken refuge in the pay phone on the ward. I asked if she wanted me to visit; she said, "Yes, bring me a sweatshirt, as it is very cold in here." She asked to speak to her dad. What a relief for both of us! Yet we were skeptical—I didn't know what to make of it, as she had not received any medication. When asked what brought about the change, she said "cognitive therapy" with a laugh. When I arrived at 4:00

p.m., she was standing by the front door to the ward. Thank You, God! We had a great meeting the next day also.

On Wednesday, June 9, an 11:00 a.m. meeting was scheduled with her and the social worker (Joyce). She wanted to discuss the option of a possible early retirement. Meanwhile, her supervisor from Verizon had emailed to say an 11:00 a.m.–7:00 p.m. opening was available in the office. Dee was pleased to consider that as another option. Later that evening, Medlife, her insurance agent, called for her. I informed them that she was not available but rather hospitalized. They told me that I would need a letter of authorization to have the case discussed with me.

On Thursday, June 10, at 1:30 p.m.,
Dee had called several times, asking me to bring warm clothing, as temp was only fifty. I also had the note ready for her signature. Things went well the rest of that weekend.

On Monday, June 14, she was discharged from the hospital around 11:00 a.m. She was waiting for me by the front desk. We stopped to fill prescriptions, and she treated her dad to a sub and bought a small pizza for me. Great!

On Tuesday, June 15, she was set to start a day program at Westwood Lodge. She went over and did the paperwork to start the program the next day. She said she had a good day.

On Thursday, June 17, I dropped her off and picked her up for an appointment we had with her doctor at 4:00 p.m. We arrived a bit early; by now, she was exhibiting those manic traits of trying to squeeze too much into the allotted time frame. A discussion was had on what approach should be taken to ensure her future well-being. She only wanted to take Haldol; I was quite concerned about the side effects. Again, Lord, we need Your guidance. I became a bit concerned when she didn't call during her lunch break on Friday.

We met with her doctor again on June 25; by now, she wanted to try a new med, whereas her doctor strongly insisted why try something new when her current drugs had worked for ten years. She was not prepared for the stern lecture she received that day—still she was not convinced.

On June 28, 2010, I met with her case manager at the day program. My assessment was that my daughter was being a bit confrontational and I was not sure if she was making progress. The next day, I left for Alabama, praying that things would go well with her and her dad. I had a wonderful trip. She returned to work on July 12, 2010. She called twice while on her way home. Things went well; she did comment that the first day back was always the hardest.

On December 3, 2010, my fear was back. She was slipping. I suspected this around Thanksgiving—her attitude and irrational thinking. After work, she stated that she had a big fight with her supervisor. That was a sure sign. Maybe the stress of changing her hours might have caused her to spiral downward. She refused to be controlled (her way of thinking).

On December 11, 2010, we met with her therapist, who was also baffled by the personality change. She said she would speak with the doctor. There was nothing we could do. My child stated that she was glad that she could finally stand up for herself after fifty-one years. The supervisor and I had become enemies. Lord, give me strength. We survived somehow. Thank God for a few good years.

It is now April 24, 2013, and what I suspect to be the beginning of another downward spin … She has been having problems with her neck and legs for some time; her doctor referred her to a neurologist. I don't know who decided it was caused by the meds. But right away, she is stopping the Haldol. Lord, help us!

2013

2013

October 28, 2013

My fears are being manifested. My child is definitely on a downward spin. I contacted the doctor to see if anything could be done. He suggested she come in to see him. Lord, help me to get through to her! I feel so sorry for her supervisors in the workplace. See Psalm 138:7,

"Though I walk in the midst of trouble, thou wilt revive me. Thou shall stretch forth thine hand against the wrath of mine enemiesand thy right hand shall save me.

2014

2014

April 13, 2014
This has been a very difficult year, six months into the new year. I have seen a little improvement, but things are not up to par in her demeanor and behavior.

I can't mention the workplace to her. The loud music is constantly blasting—especially the song "Happy by Pharrell Williams!

April 27, 2014
I heard that she had been suspended from the job (insubordination); I was not told when this transpired. I called her doctor who had no insight on her behavior or how she would manage her medication (she would not adhere to his suggestions). It was revealed in her next visit with her doctor that I had spoken with him. Of course, she was not happy about that.

May 14, 2014
Bomb shed! She began annual leave from job. I was informed that she was making plans for day treatment. While on leave, she was busy looking into public housing in the Boston area.

May 21, 2014

Her dad left for a trip to Alabama. She drove him to the airport. En route back home, during a discussion, I said, "Whatever a mother does is done out of love." This comment blew her mind about seeing me; she yelled so loudly until I was fearful of an accident on Highway 95. We had nothing more to say en route; by the time we got home, she was almost back to her new normal self. I was truly grateful that she had been removed from the workplace before other charges and allegations began.

May 23, 2014

She had got enrolled in a program at Westwood Lodge. We were scheduled a family meeting, which turned into a disaster. She walked out and dropped out of the program. My life had become a living hell.

May 27, 2014

I was talking with someone on the phone; she overheard her name being mentioned, which resulted in another blowout. To cool off a bit, I jumped into my car and drove down the street (about thirty minutes); when I returned, she had packed a bag and left. She did call back to say she was okay and was with friends. She also called her father and brother to say she was okay but would not be returning home tonight. This was the first time for such an episode. Lord, help me to hold out!

The next morning at six, I received this call:
"Did you sleep well last night?"
My answer was, "No, I did not."
She said, "Well, I slept very well."
I asked where are you.
"Don't worry about it. Goodbye."

She returned home after two nights away. To this day, I have no idea as to where she was. The past few weeks were horrible. I had no idea of her activities. The following week, she would leave home around 6:30 a.m.—returning around 10:00 p.m. or later. Lord, keep her safe!

On June 18, 2014, I saw a small ray of light; I was hopeful that this was the beginning of a turnaround—not so. By Sunday, I was faced with something that had never happened before. She left home early Saturday evening and did not return until 3:00 a.m. on Sunday—no explanation; she was being in control of her own life.

By July 2, things appeared to be well enough for me to keep my planned trip to Alabama (July 2–9, 2014). While I was away, things went downhill again. I almost cut the trip short but decided that I would stay since we were not allowed to be a part of her life anyway.

Notes taken on July 4, 2014, at 5:40 a.m. (Gainesville, Alabama)

Dear, God! Please help us. Things are not good back home. My child has fallen back into deep despair. I feel for her father, having to cope with this alone. I realize that there is nothing either of us can do. I have dealt with this disease many years but never witnessed this current behavior. She goes in and out of psychoses (without warning). Her brother warned that this would happen until she is stabilized. The blockers in the brain are firing off—like firecrackers being thrown against a brick wall. A few days ago, she described it as "little dot seeping out of the brain." What a terror this must be. I can only imagine what she is going through. In spite of her suffering, she has fought a tremendous battle. Only You, God, can help her. Give all of us strength to climb these mountains. When her thoughts were clearer, she indicated that she wished her being evaluated at McLean Hospital (one of the best in the country) could serve to help someone else.

I arrived home the evening of July 9, 2014. She did not arrive home until midnight. Around 9:00 p.m., she called to check in but would not reveal her whereabouts. The next morning, I was assigned the task of dropping her off at the bus stop. She did the driving, and I was not permitted to say anything to her, as she was in her own world. The same thing occurred when I picked her up that evening at the train station. Later that evening, she was bouncing off the wall, dancing and making faces (she even spat at me). Around 10:30 p.m., she came to my door and said, "Call the cops." I realized this was my opportunity. She was calling out for help. I made the call quietly and quickly, as I had been in contact with the Walpole police a couple of times beforehand. We decided I would not make her aware until their arrival—in case she would take off. Just as the patrol car pulled into my driveway, I opened her door and told her that the officers were coming to transport her to the ER. Without a word, she got out of bed and began to get dressed. About five officers and ambulance arrived. She was leaving peacefully until she got outside and saw the ambulance. At that point, she became enraged and refused to go in the ambulance (she was not going to pay that bill). The officer mentioned handcuffs, which she welcomed by tending out both hands to be cuffed. She was led away as I turned to go back inside to follow by car to the hospital. When I arrived in the ER with the attending doctor, all hell broke loose. I turned and left the room quickly. She was kept there overnight as they sought placement for her. I had suggested she be sent to McLean. She refused to submit to the medical requirements for McLean and was sent to Bournewood Hospital instead.

On Saturday, July 12, 2014, I received a phone call from her, citing a long list of personal things I *must* bring her. I had to stop at Best Buy on my way to buy a CD player for her. These things had to be inspected at the desk. She was informed that CD players were not allowed, but since it had a radio, she was allowed to keep it (big mistake). She went through each piece of garment, checking the sizes; anything that did not meet her specification had to be taken back home. This was not to be a visit only to drop off things.

Early Sunday morning, I received a phone call from her seeking a telephone number. There was to be no conversation. Her instructions were to keep it simple. She demanded I bring her a blue hoodie sweatshirt instead of the one I had left for her.

On Monday, at 5:00 a.m., she called to request I drop off a package (not for a visit/conversation), so I refused to go. I received another call on Tuesday morning. She was still keeping it simple—drop-off package only. My niece from Alabama was in town to visit; she and I went to the hospital. My daughter received the package but did not wish to communicate with us. She apologized to my niece. Meanwhile, I placed a call to her psychiatrist.

On Wednesday (July 16, 2014), at 5:20 a.m., she called to say, "Don't call me. Don't call me. I will do the calling." And she hung up. Around noontime, she called again to get her brother's phone number. I was forbidden to give her number to anyone.

Her orginal doctor called to say he had left a message for the doctor at the hospital, after the doctor at the hospital returned his call., her original doctor called again to report that my daughter was still refusing to cooperate with every one. And the confidential aspects prevented them from giving out unauthorized info.

On Friday (July 18, 2014), I had absolutely no contact (even negative info was better than hearing nothing). I dialed the phone on the ward; it was either not answered or she refused to take the call. "Lord, help me through this ordeal."

On Saturday (July 19, 2014), I called the nurses' station. I was told that she was sleeping.

On Sunday (July 20, 2014), at 5:00 a.m., she called—still keeping it real. "Don't call me. I will call you."

The afternoon of July 21, 2014 (Monday), I was called to testify before a panel of administrators and judge at the hospital regarding the need to medicate. She refused to attend. After the hearing, I went to the ward to see her. She threw me out the door. The next morning, at six thirty, she called to say, "Don't call me. I will call you." Around 7:00 a.m., she called to say that she was at Brigham and Women's Hospital. She rattled off a long list of things to bring along with the Koran. I later discovered that she had been brought in during the night with an emergency medical issue. One cannot imagine what it is like not being able to get any information without the patient's permission.

At 9:00 p.m., I called the hospital to see if she had been discharged. I was told she would be sent back to Bournewood sometime before morning. Meanwhile, I still did not know what happened. I was thinking it might have had something to do with the medication (Haldol) and noted that I would speak to the doctor ASAP.

On July 24, 2014, shortly after 6:00 p.m., I received a call from her. "Hi, Mom. I am much better."

I made my first visit on Friday, July 21. We had a nice visit on Friday and Saturday. I did not visit on Sunday. She called around 7:00 a.m. on Monday. She spoke very softly as not to disturb the other clients. Things went well for that week.

I did not visit again until Monday, August 4. I discovered she had been taken off the Haldol on Saturday. What a big mood change. The doctor stated that she was hyper and they might have to revert back to Haldol. The next morning, I received a friendly call from her at 7:20 a.m. At 10:30 a.m., all hell broke loose. The doctor had informed her of our conversation. She was livid and was back in a very agitated mood. She called to say she was not moving to Alabama with us. She quickly hung up the telephone. *Lord, have mercy!* This whole ordeal had been unlike anything I had witnessed before. I spoke with her social worker; they, too, were at a loss and did not know what was causing this. I prayed for peace for her tormented mind.

I had no contact with her that weekend. On Monday (August 11, 2014), at 7:00 a.m., she called to see if I was scheduled to pick her up. I was dumbfounded; how could she be discharged in this state of mind? I was forbidden to interfere with her business. After all, she was age fifty-five! She was not coming home but going to a relative's home instead. In a state of disbelief, I called the nurses' station. The nurse I spoke with had been off that weekend and didn't know what was going on. She promised to call me as soon as the social worker or nurse arrived. At 8:35 a.m., there was still no call, so I called again and was told that the parties were in a meeting and I would hear from the social worker after their meeting.

Meanwhile, I spoke with the relative whom she was going to live with. She had been in contact with the hospital regarding transportation. Shortly after 9:30 a.m., the social worker called me to say an arrangement had been made and my daughter was being discharged and was being picked up by this relative. I asked to speak with the doctor, as I didn't believe that they would just throw a sick mind to the wolves like this. They had concluded that my daughter was functioning at her best. No additional improvement was expected. *Wow*, what a kick in the stomach!

The relative brought her by my home to pick up some things. She decided to stay. Things went fairly well for the next week.

On August 22, 2014, at 12:30 a.m., she was getting up for the day. It occurred to me that she was slipping again. I worried about her new medicine. It was not working well for her.

What do you do when you have done all that you can do? Well, you just stand!

Things went fairly well for September and October, but I was never at ease anymore. She put in her retirement papers. By Thanksgiving (November 27, 2014), I discovered that she had stopped taking Haldol. I was being nagged constantly; she even informed me that she had changed her will.

2015

The following months were very stressful. I developed health issues and had emergency surgery in April 2015. For a while, she was quite helpful during this period. By late summer, she had become very disturbed. I called her doctor, seeking assurance that there was still hope for her. Not so. It was sad to accept the realization that the love and trust that existed between parent and child was probably lost forever. Her doctor supported the notion that to move out on her own might be the best thing for her. She had been seeking housing (subsided housing) in Massachusetts for quite a while now. She did not realize that her source of income was far above that level. Near the end of September 2015, I was back in the hospital for a second (planned) surgery; she had developed a selfish and "self only" attitude. She did not visit the hospital or rehab center and informed us that we would be on our own. She did drive me home, and that was the extent of her help. Her father and I both had surgery at the same time. She refused to assist in any manner. Things had got to be very sad at this point. She stopped speaking to us. She would leave home as early as 6:00 a.m. and return around 10:00 p.m.—no contact with us at all. She had transferred all her calls to her cell phone, shutting us out of her life completely. Her fifty-sixth birthday was on November 20, 2015. I purchased her a twenty-five-dollar gift card along with a photo that was taken with her while I was in recovery after my first surgery; she ripped the photo up and threw it in the trash. I don't know if she used the gift card or not. She was not around for Thanksgiving or our Kwanzaa celebration.

On December 2015, we had become her no. 1 enemies. How much can a mother's heart take? On Christmas Eve, I attempted to give her a gift from her father (two supermarket gift cards). She took it and threw it in the trash, stating, "The only gift I want from you all is my space." She packed her usual lunch and water and took off for the evening without a word at 4:00 p.m. It was now three, Christmas morning, and still no word from her. At 6:00 a.m., I contacted the police department for help and advice. They tracked her cell phone to a tower in the South-end. I made another call to the police station. I was told there was nothing they could do.

But as God would intervene, an officer called later to say they would make contact with Boston PD to pinpoint her car. She had since moved to Cambridge. They would be on the lookout for her. At 6:00 p.m., she arrived home, no explanation. She went directly to her room. I called the PD to call off the search. A few minutes later, an officer knocked on my door to DEE, in order to do a well-being check. With my heart pounding (knowing that she would go off), I begged him to take my word for it. Not wishing to cause more problems, he wished me a Merry Christmas and left. These results provided a great deal of relief, ever so painful.

2016

2016

January 2016—this had been a month of living hell. There had been absolutely no communication between us. On January 27, I received a call from Wrentham Police Department—my daughter had been sent to Norwood Hospital for evaluation. Thank God for the intervention. After several calls to the hospital, I was provided general information (after assuring them that the police department had contacted me). I was able to speak with the in-charge nurse on her ward and dropped off a change of clothes for her with the nurse. Later I received a call from my child stating that she needed no clothing. She advised me not to come near her. Unable to get any information on her well-being (per patient's request) for a whole week, I engaged an attorney. Due to bad weather and cancellations of court hearing twice along with the doctor's opinion that client would adhere to needed medication. It wasn't long before that hope vanished, and a hearing was scheduled for February 16, 2016. What a disaster; it was almost unbelievable that someone could be so deranged and emaciated. Later that evening, after being medicated, she called—sounding almost normal. The very next day, she called again with a very different story. She warned me not to attempt any contact with her. There was absolutely no contact until Saturday, February 20, 2016; she called to say I could visit and bring clothes and mail (visiting

71

hours were 2:00 p.m.–4:00 p.m.). It was a very brief visit, as she soon became very irate and ordered me to leave and not come back the next day (Sunday). I received another shocker on Monday; I discovered that she had closed an account that was in both names at the bank. Lord, what a war. I compared it with fighting in the jungle of some foreign country. I called the attorney to drop the guardianship. He was in agreement after seeing how she performed at the hearing.

It was not until March 5 that I was able to make contact with her again. I visited the ward but was disappointed that I was not allowed to say a word, while she was very talkative with the other patients and their guests; in her way of thinking, I was not in existence. So I soon left the hospital. I was scheduled to meet with her doctor and social worker on Monday. I was sure it was to make plans for a discharge. Lord, the pain is back in the heart. Can/should she be allowed to return home? Please, Lord, show me the path that I must take. She was discharged on Friday, March 11, 2016; she refused to allow me to pick her up, so she was transported by cab. Things at home went fairly decent while adjusting to normal routine. She was set up in a two-week day program. We had another snowstorm on March 21; lo and behold, she cleared my car. She is slowly grasping the many evil things and heartaches she has caused us—but will not be held responsible. I must learn to leave her alone; it is impossible to reason with her.

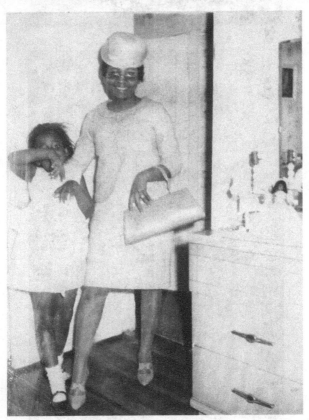

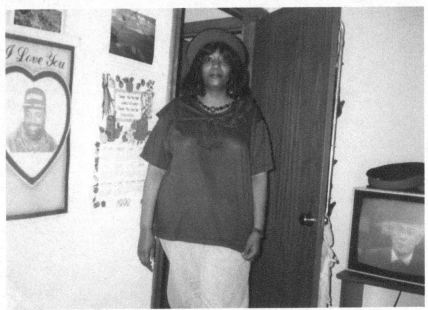

2020

January 20, 2020. I have been on a hiatus since my last writing of March 2016 Dee moved to an apartment in Cambridge, Massachusetts, in 2017. We did not put any pressure on her, so she finally found a studio apartment in Cambridge, Massachusetts. It was a very expensive location but had all the amenities that she was looking for. Once she was all set, we began to make arrangements to relocate back to Alabama. She was very happy in her studio apartment in Central Square. From that time (2017) until 2020, things went very well. She would visit us regularly and had begun to stay as long as two/three weeks at a time. As she got older, she began to appreciate the mundane life. She had shared with friends that she might consider moving to Alabama. She had scheduled trips for April and July 2020. During the two years that we were apart, she had not missed a single day from calling us. Each morning at six, the phone would ring. "Hello, Mom, have you made it to the kitchen yet?" She knew my schedule: get up and shower then off to the kitchen to make breakfast for her dad before taking off to the gym at 7:00 a.m. Her last visit was October 2019; she spent three weeks with us.

February 28, 2020 (Saturday)—the first sign of problems, she didn't call at 6:00 a.m. today. After waiting a while and she was not answering her phone, her dad sent a cousin out to Cambridge to check on her. She was not home. When she was reached later through a neighbor, she became very angry, calling from the neighbor's phone (as she had lost her phone); we were told never to do that again. We did not hear from her again that weekend. Finally, her phone stopped ringing, and the calls were going directly to voice mail.

The next few days were sheer torture; we were unable to make contact with her, fearing that another episode was in the making. I booked a flight to Boston (March 5, 2020) and spent the night with the cousin; the next day, we went to her apartment but were unable to gain access. I began calling her doctor's office and spoke with the secretary who stated that she would call me back after speaking to the doctor whom she said was not available at the time. I waited all day to no avail. Around 3:30 p.m., I called the office again and got voice mail. Meanwhile, I called her original doctor's office and learned that he was on leave until March 19. Meanwhile, news broke about the pandemic in the USA. My son called from Maryland to tell me that I should try to get the next flight out of Boston, as the states were shutting down. I was able to book on American Airlines. Upon landing in Birmingham, I was informed that my husband's sister had passed in Saginaw, Michigan.

Meanwhile, in the middle of the night, I remembered Atty. Hilliard who had represented me in court hearing over the years. I was able to reach him on my first attempt. I emailed him the pertinent information. I also contacted the building office manager at her complex. With the weekend approaching, I cannot relive the frustration of following days. The world was being informed that we were in the midst of a virus outbreak.

On Monday morning (March 16), I called the office manager; she reported that Phyllis had not been seen over the weekend. She would do a well-being check at the apartment. At 11:00 a.m., I received a call that my daughter, Phyllis, was found deceased in her apartment.

I made necessary arrangements for a flight to Boston and arrived at Logan Airport at 12:30 a.m. on Tuesday. I was picked up at the airport by cousins (the Goodman family). Early Tuesday morning, we headed to Cambridge. I thought I would stay at her apartment, which was in total disarray. I made an appointment to meet with the funeral home director at 3:00 p.m. My son arrived on Wednesday (March 18, 2020). We were unable to view the body. There were tons of work to be done. The world was in an uproar; the coronavirus scare was taking over the nation. It took several days to clear out the apartment, with help from family members. The situation was becoming more severe by the minute. By Friday, we had cleared the apartment, and we were able to book a flight back to Alabama. My son and I left Boston on Saturday. He was driving my daughter's car back to Maryland. Meanwhile, they had begun shutting down airports and roadways. With an undesirable pain in the heart, I made it home safely. Thank God, Pruitt seemed okay. I had never felt so alone and deeply saddened as when I realized that my child died *alone* in her apartment. It was at this point that I realized that the mental health and privacy system need to change. We being in Alabama and no one being able to gain access to her (without her consent), shy of having to call the police department to do a well-being check.

About this time, the entire nation was in an uproar over the pandemic—even as President Trump downplayed it and withheld the facts. The pain that followed was indescribable. We were being told that the virus was no big deal or it would magically disappear. Meanwhile, every office within the country began to shut down. (March 16, 2020) the day my daughter's body was discovered. The president's message to the public was "Just get back to work with or without a mask." It was impossible to reach anyone via telephone. I began trying to notify the many sectors that had to be notified of her death. On April 1, 2020, I made contact with an individual in the Benefits Office at Verizon, which gave me a little relief knowing that they were working on the case.

It was very difficult to get information from the funeral director on having her ashes sent to us in Alabama. He wasn't sure if the shipping problem was with the cemetery or the postal service restrictions regarding COVID-19. He even suggested we pick up the remains (Lord Jesus).

It was on April 7, 2020, that I made contact with Debra Goldman of Wayland, Massachusetts, regarding an article she had written for the local paper on mental illness. She also has a brother with health issues. We instantly connected; after hearing about the difficultly I was having with the funeral home, she offered to pick up the urn and mail it to me. (Isn't God great!) Meanwhile, my son and I were checking into the shipping holdup. We learned that there was a special shipping kit to be used through the postal service. We ordered the kit and had it mailed directly to the funeral home director. He then began to take action. The shipment was made to the Gandy Funeral Home, Eutaw, Alabama. The nightmarish sudden death provided many exhaustive obstacles—many caused by the pandemic. I was mentally unable to claim the urn from Gandy's on its arrival, so I was assured it would be safe and presented no problem for them to hold as long as needed. What a relief—the joy of that moment helped to reduce the pain of my loss. I finally claimed the urn on October 15, 2020.

Meanwhile, as I was copying/printing the messages and condolences from the web page, I found in the midst of those pages an undated and unsigned meditation experiment done by my daughter at the assumed meditation center in Cambridge, Massachusetts, shortly before her death titled "The Pebbles." How it got into my hands remains a puzzle. I called the meditation center to see if they sent it. They did not, and they were not aware of her death. I will share the contents of that exercise later.

July 2020—I am having a difficult time trying to continue the new chapter to my story. The loss can never be defined or clarified. There are so many unanswered questions: How and when did she die? Was it from the COVID-19? The only thing I know for sure is that she died alone in her apartment (not sure when—only that her body was discovered on March 16, 2020, by the complex manager to whom I am forever grateful).

Turning Pain into a Purpose

Many years ago, I conceived the notion of starting a Black history library at my home in Gainesville, Alabama. On one of my trips to Africa, I met a fellow traveler who was in the editing business for a book publishing company. She had access to many editions that she started donating to me. I kept all of them in my home. So after the loss of my daughter, I decided it was time to bring this idea to fruition. The next few months were spent on setting up the Phyllis D. Pruitt Memorial Library.

On September 6, 2020, we had a successful memorial library dedication supported by the entire community. Weeks later, as I sit in the library, revisiting happy memories from collages, books, and other keepsakes of Phyllis, I realize I must get back to pen and paper if I am going to bring closure to this story. I find much solace in reading/rereading the many kind condolences, letters, and many acts of kindness shown by those that knew her well.

December 25, 2020, Christmas Day: It is a bright sunny day; temp's in fifties. Yet it is a sad day for me. I returned to my writing of a Christmas spent many years ago. It helps to watch the Chicago Independence Miles Concert. ABC TV did a special edition (GMA3). What a relief to watch something other than President Trump and COVID-19, which has dominated the airways for months now. It is heartbreaking to learn that the death toll has reached over two hundred thousand.

2021

January 6, 2021: The attack on the Capitol by Trump's followers is almost as painful as the news of my sudden loss. Lord, what have we come to? It brings to mind the scripture 2 Chronicles 7:14:

> IF my people which are called by my name
> shall humble themselves, and pray, and seek my
> face and turn from their wicked ways.; Tthen will
> I hear from Heaven, and will forgive their sins
> and will heal their land."

Heal the land, Lord. Heal the land!

January 18, 2021, Dr. Martin Luther King Jr. celebration

I know I must finish this story. Several times I have attempted to write at least a paragraph—I just jot down a few words and put it aside again.

Each day I visit the library for two hours or so to read or just find peace in the quietness and memories. I acquired this habit over the years of having to visit her daily each time she was hospitalized. I pray that the sharing of my story will help someone along the way. I have shed many tears and are shedding them as I write this. But if it can help some desperate soul, then the shed tears will be worthwhile. You see, I traveled this journey almost alone (except when Christ carried me). Since her death, I was given the book *I Wasn't Ready to Say Goodbye* by Brook Noel and Pamela D. Blair, PhD, to read. The book has been helpful for coping under many situation during the grieving process. It has now been one year and one month since my daughter's death. I think of her every day, but it is not every day that I shed tears. There is truth in these words:

> Death leaves a heartache that no one can heal,
> but love leaves a memory no one can steal."
> (Anonymous)

But *God*!

Let me share with you a piece (undated and unsigned) that she authored in her last days on earth during a meditation session.

The Pebble

> I had difficulty doing this exercise and it was hard
> to be the actual pebble. My mind kept seeing
> the pebble as a separate entity. When I was able
> to see myself as the pebble, I saw myself as a
> pebble in a clear stream. I was able to sink to the
> bottom of the stream peacefully without resisting
> the water ...
>
> A love one who had died
> —I started thinking about my aunt who passed
> away recently. Disturbing thoughts went through
> my head; I began to wonder what the real

meaning of life was. Thoughts that everything is impermanent surfaced. I began to think that everything is irrelevant. I began to get sad. I began to breathe faster. I had to consciously slow my breathing down. I began to become fearful. A lot of issues came up for me while doing this exercise. Thoughts of my own death surfaced and I began to realize that death is real and unavoidable. I thought of death before but never meditated on it. Doing this exercise made me do a fearless inventory of my feelings regarding the seriousness of death. I began to wonder if I was living to my fullest because tomorrow is not promised. Some anxiety surfaced within me, however, I looked at these negative feelings and realized I was just feeling feelings. I half smiled and like the book suggested and a peaceful feeling came over me, the sadness lifted and for a moment I accepted death.

Photo Gallery

About to face that New England weather

Getting ready to hang out

Attending a workshop

Smiling to help brighten the holidays

getting ready for African celebration (1992)

Oh Happy Day

The Happy Family" Photo, (left to right)
Aaron Jr. Mom Bertha, Phyllis & Aaron Sr.

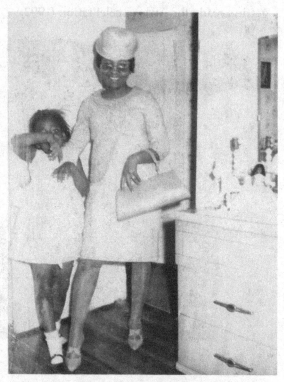

Getting ready for church (1960s)

getting ready for "The Easter Parade" 1960's

College graduation 1982

getting ready for "The Easter Parade" 1960s

College graduation 1987

9 781664 181021